A Family Tradition Christmas Cookbook

BY

Shirley Rene Janisse

© 2013 All Rights Reserved. No part of this publication may be reproduced in any form or by any means, including scanning, photocopying, or otherwise without prior written permission of the copyright holder.

www.168Publishing.com

Table of Contents

About the Author 5
Introduction: 7
An Old Fashioned Christmas Breakfast 8
    Overnight Cinnamon and Raisin Bread Pudding 10
    Yummy Baked Sausage and Egg Casserole 12
Favorite Homemade Christmas Decorations: 14
    Hanging Orange Clove Balls 15
    Homemade Tree Ornaments 17
Christmas Candies 19
    Delightful Divinity 21
    Great Grandmas Chocolate-Walnut Fudge 23
    Dreamy Creamy Peanut Butter Fudge 25
    Old Fashioned Peanut Butter Brittle 27
    Hard Candy Peppermints 28
    Christmas Nut Caramels 30
Christmas Cookies 32
    Chocolate Chip Cookies 33
    Perfect Peanut Butter Cookies 35
    Spicy Ginger Snaps 37
    Pecan Snowballs 39
    Decorative Christmas Sugar Cookies 41
Homemade Pies, Puddings, and Other Wonderful Desserts 43
    Just Can't Beat It Basic Pie Crust 45

Raisin Pie	48
Classic Mincemeat Pie	50
Meringue	53
Cherished Chocolate Meringue Pie	55
Lemony Lemon Meringue Pie	57
Extremely Palatable Pecan Pie	59
First Choice Cherry Pie	61
Amazing Apple Pie	63
Perfectly Pleasant Pumpkin Roll	65
Can't Be Beat Banana Pudding	67
Mammas Seventy Five Dollar Persimmon Pudding	69
Irresistible Cherry Jubilee	71
Over The Top Red Velvet Cake	73
Colorful Christmas Cake	75
Z-licious Zucchini Bread	78
Best Ever Banana Nut Bread	80
Christmas Buffet	82
Glorious Glazed Ham	86
Creamy Chicken and Fluffy Drop Dumplings	88
Bodacious Beef and Noodles	90
Succulent Swedish Meatballs	92
Doubly Yummy Yeast Rolls	95
Lovely Layered Salad	97
Wonderful and Fruity Waldorf Salad	99
Best Ever Broccoli Salad	101

About the Author

Shirley Rene (Richardson) Janisse was born in Bloomington, Indiana in 1961 to Henry Lee and Elva Irene (Brown) Richardson. She has a total of seven siblings; in which three are brothers and four are sisters. Two brothers and one sister were already more than thirteen years older than her when she was born, and by the time she was six she had already became an aunt three times since they had married and began families of their own .

To date, her brothers and sisters have made her an aunt to eight nieces and eleven nephews. Most of them refer to her as their "Favorite Aunt", citing that she is fun to be around and has a very creative imagination.

Shirley has two grown sons, Timothy and Jacob, and has three grandchildren. She married her husband Norman in 1995 and they currently reside in New Port Richey, Florida.

Her first attempt at writing began when she was twelve and she wrote an entire Christmas play which starred her nieces and nephews. Her love for writing became even more apparent at the age of fifteen when she was asked by her

Youth Pastor to produce a monthly news letter for the Church she attended.

In High School she excelled in English Literature and she dreamed of attending college and taking courses in Journalism, but the lack of funds and raising a family took her down a different path. After years of trying her hand at various things in which none of them ever seemed fulfilling, the desire to write became an all consuming fire.

In 2010, she quit her job at the factory where she had been working as a medical parts assembler for over ten years. She purchased a computer and began her writing career online as a Ghostwriting Freelance writer, often underbidding the projects due to her lack of a college degree. It didn't take her long though to produce a reputable profile as a Freelance writer in which she was offered more projects than she could possibly handle.

In 2011, she began being recognized as a published author when she had her poem titled "Time" published by World Poetry Movement in a coffee-table edition called "Stars in Our Hearts". Since then she has had several accomplishments, including her "How to Teach Sunday School… A Step by Step Guide" published by How Expert Press, and her first Children's book titled "Dylan and the Dungeon Dragon" published by Amazons KDP Select as a Kindle edition.

Shirley has currently been producing Cookbooks. Most of her inspiration comes from family recipes that have been passed down through four generations. Although Shirley became a professional writer, her four sisters' work as professional cooks and her mother recently retired after cooking professionally for over 40 years.

Introduction:

This is not your average Christmas Cookbook, but rather something special and full of Christmas Tradition. A Cookbook, in which will not only supply your family with some great recipes to make your Christmas's memorable, but also something worth passing down to the next generation, keeping this Family Christmas Tradition alive for ages to come.

An Old Fashioned Christmas Breakfast

Our Family Christmas Tradition actually began with my great-great-great grandparents on my mother's side who raised a very large family. Christmas Day always began with a breakfast consisting of Homemade Bread Pudding and a Sausage and Egg Casserole that was prepared the night before and placed inside a brick oven that was built by my great-great-great grandfather. Of course back then the bread for the pudding came from homemade bread. The sausage came from the pigs that were raised on the farm, and then eggs had to be gathered from the henhouse. Since there were 14 children in that family, it took a lot of hens to produce the amount of eggs that were needed.

When I was a young child, my Mother prepared the Bread Pudding and the Sausage and Egg Casserole on Christmas Eve, just as her mother had, and her grandmother had, and her great grandmother had! Of course by that time, she was able to purchase the ingredients at the local market.

So when it came time for me to continue this breakfast tradition with my own small family, I also continued preparing mine on Christmas Eve. It just made sense not to have to spend all morning putting it together while my children were anxiously waiting to open their presents. Instead, I would just pop it in the oven, and let it bake while my family opened their presents.

I always found these dishes to be very delectable, and I believe your family will delight in them almost as much as the presents that they will receive. And since they are so tasty, it won't be as hard as you think to pull your kids away from their presents long enough to enjoy a hearty nutritious breakfast!

Overnight Cinnamon and Raisin Bread Pudding

Made from day old bread that was bought from the local bread store, this bread pudding is a delightful breakfast treat on Christmas Morning. Since it is refrigerated overnight, the cinnamon has the opportunity to be more absorbed into the pudding and the raisins make this pudding even more delightful.

Ingredients:

- 1 large loaf of French bread
- 3 cups milk
- 6 large eggs
- 2 Tbsp. sugar
- ½ Tsp. ground cinnamon
- 1 Tablespoon vanilla
- ½ cup raisins
- 1 Tbsp. butter

Directions:

1. Grease a shallow 2 ½ quart casserole dish.

2. Break up bread into cube size pieces and place in casserole dish.

3. Add raisins into bread cubes and mix until evenly distributed.

4. In a large mixing bowl, combine milk, eggs, sugar, cinnamon and vanilla.

5. Pour mixture over bread mixture evenly.

6. Cover with casserole dish lid and refrigerate overnight.

7. Preheat oven to 325°F.

8. Remove lid and dot bread pudding with butter.

9. Bake for 45 minutes to an hour or until light golden brown.

Yummy Baked Sausage and Egg Casserole

This casserole is easy to make and can easily be baked in the oven at the same time as the bread pudding, making your Christmas breakfast a snap.

Ingredients:

- 8 slices of bread, toasted, then crumbled
- 6 eggs
- 2 cups milk
- 1 onion, diced
- ½ tsp. salt
- ½ tsp. black pepper
- 1 Tbsp. bacon bits
- ½ large green pepper, diced
- 1 pound sausage
- 1 pound grated Colby cheese
- ¼ cup butter

Directions:

1. In skillet, cook sausage until well done and drain off oil.

2. Grease a 9 x 13 inch baking pan.

3. In large bowl, mix toasted and crumbled bread pieces, diced onions and peppers, and bacon bits and pour out into baking pan.

4. Cover bread crumb mixture with cheese.

5. In a separate mixing bowl, beat eggs, salt, pepper and milk together.

6. Pour egg mixture on top of cheese.

7. Cover with foil and refrigerate overnight.

8. Preheat oven to 325°F.

9. Remove foil and dot with butter.

10. Bake in oven for an hour or until golden brown.

Favorite Homemade Christmas Decorations:

My mother came from a large family, in which she had fifteen siblings. She grew up on a farm, and learned to cook at the early age of eight. Presents were always homemade gifts, and all the foods prepared were made from scratch. There are drawbacks from coming from a large family, one of them being that there never seems to be enough money for the things you want. There is one sure thing though, and that is that large families tend to be close knitted and know how to survive without a lot of material things. The important things seem to be family, love, faith, traditions, and the ability to cook delicious and hearty meals.

Growing up in such a large family as I did, Christmas was always made special by the love that my Mother put into every thing that she made and served to us on Christmas Day. Presents under the tree were never plentiful. We received one each and knew of the sacrifices that had been made in order for them to be purchased. Christmas decorations were made by hand and children gloried in their accomplishments.

These days, the fragrances of Christmastime are replaced by store-bought potpourri and the decorations are produced in factories. Even with all the store has to offer, nothing can ever replace the scent of these Hanging Orange-Clove Balls or the thrill of making these Homemade Tree Ornaments with your family.

Hanging Orange Clove Balls

Nothing reminds me of Christmas more than these Hanging Orange Clove Balls. The scent of Oranges mixed with cinnamon and cloves brings back pleasant Christmas memories of being a small toddler cuddled on my Mothers lap, being rocked to sleep next to a cozy fire in the fireplace with the scent from these orange balls that hung from both ends of the mantle.

Ingredients:

- 6 large oranges
- 6 rubber bands
- Container of whole cloves
- 24 cinnamon sticks
- 6 hairnets
- Nylon thread
- Darning Needle
- Green & red ribbon

Directions:

1. Place hairnet around each orange and secure open end with rubber band.

2. Using Darning needle, run 4-1 foot strands of nylon thread through each orange and through the rubber band leaving equal amounts of thread on each end of orange.

3. At the bottom of the orange, tie 1 cinnamon stick to each one of the 4 threads.

4. Pull the threads up from the top of the orange until the cinnamon sticks are just 1 inch from the bottom of the orange.

5. At the top of the orange, make a knot just above the rubber band with the thread; make a loop with the existing thread to hang the oranges by.

6. Press whole cloves into the orange and arrange them around the orange, using at least 15 per orange for maximum scent.

7. Tie green or red ribbons around rubber band area.

8. Hang oranges from ceiling or hearth. The scent of the orange-clove balls will become stronger as the days go by. I generally make these and hang them two weeks prior to Christmas.

Homemade Tree Ornaments

One of my fondest childhood memories would be making these ornaments with my mother and my younger siblings. Although the kitchen always ended up being a mess and paint tended to adhere to our clothing, mother didn't seem to mind. She was giving us a great memory, and that was a gift that could never be taken away.

Ingredients:

- 8 cups flour
- 2 cups salt
- 3 cups water
- Christmas Cookie Cutters
- Rolling pin
- Acrylic Paint
- Clear shellac
- Emery board

Directions:

1. Preheat oven to 325° F.

2. In a large mixing bowl combine the salt with the flour.

3. Gradually stir in the water until mixture forms a substance similar to putty.

4. On a lightly floured surface, knead dough for 5 minutes.

5. Using a rolling pin, roll out dough to 1/2 inch.

6. Cut ornaments with cookie cutters. Cut each ornament out as close as ¼ inch from each ornament as not to waste the dough.

7. Place ornaments on ungreased cookie sheet and bake for ½ hour.

8. Cool ornaments and place them on a covered table to paint.

9. Using an emery board, carefully file down any rough edges.

10. Paint ornaments with Acrylic paint on front and sides and then allow paint to dry. When paint has dried, turn ornaments over and paint the other side.

11. Apply clear shellac to ornaments on all sides to protect them and they will last for years to come.

Christmas Candies

I was 24 the last time that my family all got together under the roof of the small house that I grew up in for Christmas Dinner. By this time, my parents had become grandparents 10 times. With my siblings gathering together with their spouses and their children, a total of 27 persons, 3- 8ft. tables, and 1 large Christmas tree surrounded by presents that covered a three foot area around the tree were all squeezed in what used to seem like a large living room.

Even more crowded was the kitchen where 8 women desperately tried to prepare the Christmas Dinner, while practically stepping on top of each other, and 4 young toddlers hanging on their mothers legs crying for attention.

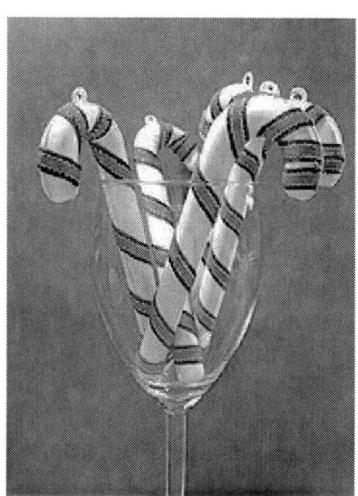

Needless to say, my Mother decided that year that it would be the last time we would get together for Christmas at home. We would be renting a hall the next time, and everyone would bring a dish. We would no longer be exchanging store-bought gifts (it was becoming extremely costly) and we would all make candies or goodie plates to pass out for gifts.

And so the Tradition of making Christmas Candies and Cookies and sharing them with our family began. And because it was such a large family, and we were all working outside the home, we had to begin making these candies and cookies well in advance. Two weeks in advance. The great thing about these candies and cookies is that they will stay fresh even if you have to make yours weeks ahead of Christmas.

Note: It is vital that you use a candy thermometer when making candy to ensure that you have reached the correct ball stages in order for the candy to set up correctly.

Delightful Divinity

Just like its name, it is divine! I won't lie, this candy takes work, but the end result is well worth it! The taste is so rich and sweet that I could never seem to eat more than one piece. Normally you will find Divinity to be white in color, but you can add red or green food coloring for a festive look.

Ingredients:

- ½ cup light corn syrup
- 2 ½ cups white sugar
- ¼ tsp. salt
- ½ cup water
- 2 egg whites
- 1 tsp. vanilla
- Food coloring (optional)
- Wax paper

Directions:

1. Lay out wax paper onto counter.

2. In a medium saucepan, combine corn syrup, sugar, salt and water.

3. Stir ingredients until sugar dissolves.

4. Cook to a hard ball stage (260° on candy thermometer).

5. Meanwhile, in a large mixing bowl, beat egg whites until they form stiff peaks. Add food coloring if desired.

6. Once they have peaked, gradually pour syrup mixture over egg whites, beating at high speed until candy holds its shape. (it usually forms after beating 4 to 5 minutes)

7. Quickly drop teaspoons of candy onto wax paper. Allow candy to cool completely.

8. Place candies on decorative platter and cover with saran wrap to keep fresh.

9. If you are making these weeks in advance, it would be best to keep them refrigerated.

Great Grandmas Chocolate-Walnut Fudge

Even though great grandma has been gone for over 50 years, she will never be forgotten. Neither will her famous chocolate-walnut fudge, which has been passed down through three generations and passed around on decorative platters every Christmas. You'll enjoy the creamy sensuous taste of this fudge so much that you'll be making it for years to come.

Ingredients:

- 6 cups sugar
- 1 ½ cups cocoa
- 3 cups milk
- 1 ½ sticks butter
- 3 tsp. vanilla
- ¾ cup chopped walnuts

Directions:

1. Grease 2-9x13 baking pans. Set aside.

2. In a large saucepan, combine sugar, cocoa and milk and stir until well blended.

3. Over medium-high heat, bring to a boil while stirring constantly.

4. Once it reaches boiling stage, stop stirring and reduce heat and simmer.

5. Place a candy thermometer in pan and continue to cook until thermometer reaches 114°C.

6. Drop a small ball into a cup of cold water to see if it forms a soft ball. Place ball between your fingers and press. If ball flattens candy has reached the desired stage.

7. Remove from heat and add butter, nuts, and vanilla.

8. Using a wooden spoon, beat fudge until it looses its sheen. (This is important, otherwise you will under beat the fudge and it will not set up properly).

9. Pour fudge into prepared pans and allow it to cool completely.

10. Cut into 1to2 inch size squares.

11. Place fudge on decorative plates and cover with plastic wrap to keep fresh. Fudge will keep good if it is made in advance and is kept in a cool dry place.

Dreamy Creamy Peanut Butter Fudge

My Mother told me that when she was a child her Grandmother made this same recipe, only they didn't have marshmallow crème available, so they made it themselves from scratch. They also didn't have evaporated milk available. So even though this recipe has been modernized and a few of the ingredients have been changed, the taste itself hasn't changed. It's still as dreamy and creamy as it was 100 years ago.

Ingredients:

- 4 cups sugar
- 1 stick butter
- 1 can evaporated milk
- 1 ¼ cup peanut butter
- 1 quart marshmallow crème
- 1 tsp. vanilla

Directions:

1. Generously butter a 9 x 13 pan and set aside.

2. Slice stick butter into pieces and place inside a large heavy-bottomed saucepan.

3. Pour in milk and sugar and bring to a rolling boil.

4. Turn heat down and boil for 10 minutes.

5. Take off heat and add remaining ingredients, stirring continuously until well blended.

6. Pour into prepared pan.

7. Cool fudge completely. Cut into desired size pieces.

8. Place on decorative platter and cover with saran wrap.

9. Fudge can be made in advance and will keep well if placed in a cool dry place.

Old Fashioned Peanut Butter Brittle

Today you would find corn syrup as an ingredient in making Peanut Butter Brittle, but not in the 1900's when this simple recipe originated. Today we also have the modern convenience of using an electric or gas stove, whereas, back then this brittle was made on top of a wood burning stove using a heavy cast iron skillet.

Ingredients:

- 6 cups sugar
- 4 cups roasted peanuts
- Butter for greasing surface

Directions:

1. Clear and clean an area on counter and butter area generously.

2. Over medium heat, place sugar in ungreased skillet and stir until sugar has melted. Sugar will lump first before melting.

3. When sugar appears pale yellow in color, pour in roasted peanuts. Stir for another minute, and then pour out onto prepared counter.

4. Cool completely, break into pieces.

5. Place in tins for storing.

Hard Candy Peppermints

One taste of these delicious minty candies is all it takes to bring back sweet memories of making this candy with my grandmother and sitting beside her while cutting it into pieces. They were precious moments that we shared while savoring such pleasant tasting candies.

Ingredients:

- 1 cup sugar
- ½ cup water
- ½ cup light corn syrup
- ¼ tsp. peppermint extract
- Green food coloring (optional)
- ¼ cup confectioners' sugar

Directions:

1. Butter a 9 x 13 inch. Pan. Set aside.

2. In a medium sized heavy bottomed pan, combine sugar, water, and corn syrup.

3. Cook mixture until sugar is dissolved while constantly stirring.

4. Once sugar is dissolved, lower the heat and cook without stirring.

5. Cook until mixture reaches the hard crack stage or 300°F on candy thermometer.

6. Remove from heat and add food coloring and peppermint extract. Stir only enough to mix.

7. Pour into prepared pan. As soon as candy has cooled enough to touch, quickly cut into pieces with scissors. Drop pieces onto a buttered platter and sprinkle with confectioners' sugar to keep them from sticking.

8. If candy cools too quickly and begins to harden where it is difficult to cut it, then place pan over hot water to soften it.

9. Place hard candy inside covered tins to keep fresh.

Christmas Nut Caramels

I might be a wee bit prejudice, but I believe my sister makes the best nut caramels ever. Unfortunately, she never seems to make enough of these delightfully chewy treats. If you have as large of a family as I have, then you might want to double this recipe.

Ingredients:

- 2 cups brown sugar
- 1 cup white sugar
- 1 cup milk
- 4 Tbsp. butter
- 1 tsp. vanilla
- 8 oz. chopped nuts
- Wax paper

Directions:

1. Butter a 9x13 in. baking pan. Set aside.

2. Cut 30-2x2 in. size pieces of wax paper.

3. In a large saucepan, combine sugars, milk, butter and vanilla.

4. Cook until waxy, stirring occasionally.

5. Remove from heat, add nuts and beat to a creamy texture.

6. Turn into prepared pan.

7. With scissors, cut into bite size pieces while warm.

8. Wrap pieces with prepared wax paper.

Christmas Cookies

When I was a little girl and four of my siblings were still living at home, we made our Christmas Cookies with our Mother on Christmas Eve. It was a grand time. Five children and one adult all cramped into a small kitchen with flour scattered everywhere. The best thing about it was we had our Mothers attention for the entire evening, since she usually worked evenings. The evening was spent baking and decorating the cookies and getting them ready for Santa. Of course, we got to sample a few along with a piping hot cup of homemade cocoa topped with marshmallows.

After we all married and began having our own families, we continued this tradition with our own children. Now our children are all married and doing the same with their children.

We still get together for Christmas, setting aside the Saturday before Christmas as the designated day. Even though it has been 28 years since we started doing this, we still continue to make goodie plates for presents. Therefore, we must also make our cookies ahead of time.

To this day, Chocolate Chip, Peanut Butter, Ginger Snaps, Snowballs and Decorated Sugar Cookies are still our favorites to make. We purchase small tins from the Dollar Store, and they keep the cookies as fresh as when we first make them.

Chocolate Chip Cookies

Oh so gooey, and oh so good, melt in your mouth chocolate cookies. Enjoy them with a mug of hot chocolate while you're piled up on the sofa next to the fireplace, watching the flames flicker as you patiently wait for Santa to arrive. Try to save some for Santa if you can, because he will love these cookies as much as you will!

Ingredients:

- 2 ¼ cups flour
- 1 tsp. salt
- 1 tsp. baking soda
- ¾ cup sugar
- ¾ cup brown sugar
- 1 cup margarine
- 2 eggs
- 1 tsp. vanilla
- 1 bag chocolate chips

Directions:

1. Preheat oven to 375°F.

2. In large bowl, mix together flour, salt, baking soda, sugars, margarine, eggs, and vanilla until mixed well.

3. Add chocolate chips and mix until evenly distributed.

4. Drop by teaspoons onto baking sheet.

5. Bake in preheated oven for 9-10 minutes.

6. Cool completely, place in tins, lining each layer with wax paper.

Perfect Peanut Butter Cookies

These Peanut Butter Cookies are not only easy to make, but they also seem to be everyone's favorite in my family. Children especially love to help in making these cookies because they are so simple to make.

Ingredients:

- 2 cups creamy peanut butter
- 2 cups sugar
- 2 eggs, beaten

Directions:

1. Preheat oven to 350°F.

2. In a large mixing bowl, mix all of the ingredients together until they form a soft ball.

3. Pinch a teaspoon of dough from the mixture and roll into a ball. Place ball onto cookie sheet.

4. Continue the process, placing each ball at least 2 inches apart. Flatten balls with the end of a glass and then make crisscrosses with the tines of a fork.

5. Bake each sheet of cookies for 8 to 10 minutes each.

6. Cool cookies and place in closed decorative tins to keep fresh.

You can add colored M&M's for a more festive look by pressing them into the top of the cookies before baking.

Spicy Ginger Snaps

There is something about the taste and smell of cinnamon, ginger and cloves that reminds me of Christmas. I guess I've always thought of these spices as winter spices. It doesn't matter how you refer to these spices, the wonderful sugary and molasses taste of these cookies are definitely a present worth getting!

Ingredients:

- 5 ¼ cups self rising flour
- 2 tsp. baking soda
- 2 tsp. cinnamon
- 2 tsp. ginger
- ½ tsp. ground clove
- 2 cups brown sugar, packed
- 1 ¼ cup unsalted butter
- 2 eggs, beaten
- ½ cup molasses

Directions:

1. In a large mixing bowl, combine together flour, soda, cinnamon, ginger and cloves. Mix well.

2. In a small bowl, beat eggs well.

3. In a medium bowl, cream together sugar and butter. Add in beaten eggs and molasses and beat until light and fluffy.

4. Pour egg mixture into the flour mixture and blend until well combined. Chill for 2 hours.

5. Preheat oven to 375°F.

6. Shape dough into 1 inch balls and then roll in granulated sugar.

7. Place dough balls about 2 inches apart on lightly greased cookie sheets.

8. Flatten balls with the end of a glass and sprinkle more sugar on top.

9. Bake in oven for 8-10 minutes. Cool completely, then place on decorative platters and cover tightly with plastic wrap.

Pecan Snowballs

I love the delicious taste of these Pecan Snowballs. They are rolled in powdered sugar to give them the appearance of a snowball, but believe me; the only place you will want to throw these delightful snowballs will be right into your mouth!

Ingredients:

- 2 cups butter
- 1 cup powdered sugar
- 2 cups finely chopped pecans
- 4 cups flour
- Extra Powdered sugar (for rolling balls to coat cookies)

Directions:

1. Preheat oven to 325°F.

2. Mix together butter, 1 cup powdered sugar, and flour. Dough will be stiff. Add in pecans and mix well.

3. Pinch a Tablespoon of dough and roll into ball.

4. Place balls onto ungreased cookie sheet. Bake for 20 minutes.

5. Cool cookies and then roll them in powdered sugar.

6. Place in tightly closed tin to keep them fresh.

Decorative Christmas Sugar Cookies

These cookies were always my favorite Christmas Cookies to make when I was a child. There was something magical about making these with my siblings and cutting them out with the cookie cutters and decorating them. Of course, we all tried to outdo each other in the decorating process and each of us believed that ours were the ones that looked the best. Of course it really didn't matter how they looked, because the taste was everything! These cookies are sweet and sugary and melt in your mouth!

Ingredients:

- 1 cup sugar
- 2 cups butter, softened at room temperature
- 2 large eggs
- ½ Tsp. salt
- 2 Tbsp. vanilla
- 4 cups flour
- Red, Green, and Blue Decorate Colored Sugar
- Christmas shaped cookie cutters

Directions:

1. In a large mixing bowl, combine sugar, butter, eggs, salt and vanilla. Mix until light and fluffy.

2. Add flour to mix and beat until well combined.

3. Wrap bowl tightly with plastic wrap and refrigerate for one hour.

4. Preheat oven to 325°F.

5. Roll dough out on lightly floured surface to ¼ inch thickness.

6. Carefully cut out shapes with cutters, cutting as close to each shape so as not to waste dough.

7. Place cookies ½ inch apart on cookie sheet and sprinkle decorate colored sugars on cookies.

8. Bake 12-15 minutes. Remove from oven and cool completely.

9. Place on decorative platter and tightly cover with plastic wrap to keep cookies fresh.

Homemade Pies, Puddings, and Other Wonderful Desserts

It wasn't long after we had decided to rent a hall for our Christmas Dinner Family gatherings that we realized that we would need a separate table just for the desserts. An 8 foot table to be exact! Our family kept growing and it seemed like each year there was a new addition. Someone had either had a new baby or was due any day.

Since our family was somewhat famous in our hometown for making delicious baked goods, it only seemed right to have these delicious baked goods available at our Christmas Dinners. My Mother had taught us how to make pies from scratch at an early age and other desserts as well. Most of these desserts were often made by her and sold at auction at her Church, often bringing in $75.00 per dessert.

Because our family had become so enormous, you would find two each of our favorite pies on the dessert table. You would find two Raisin pies, two Mincemeat pies, two Chocolate Meringue pies, two Lemon Meringue pies, two Pecan pies, two Cherry and two Apple pies! However, you will not find a pumpkin pie, because we had our fill of them the month before at Thanksgiving. You would find a Pumpkin Roll though.

And if pie was not your forte, then you could choose to have some of my Mother' famous Banana pudding or her Persimmon pudding or my sister-in- laws' Cherry Jubilee. In order to do so though, you would need to get your dessert as soon as you finished going down the huge Dinner Buffet table, or you would miss your chance of getting some, since those two desserts seem to disappear quickly!

Of course you will also find Cake on the dessert table. Red Velvet Cake is a must at Christmas, and its velvety texture on your tongue is such a delightful treat. There is also a Christmas cake, and the children seem to love it dearly. They just can't seem to resist its colorfulness on the inside.

Last, but not least, you will find Zucchini Bread and Banana Bread. And at the end of the table you can grab a jar to take home of either Apple Butter or Peach preserves that were made during the fall. So now you can see why we needed an 8 ft. table just for our desserts!

Just Can't Beat It Basic Pie Crust

It can take years of practice to make a great pie crust, and I can surely attest to that. I had tried several pie crust recipes over the years and sometimes I gave in and just bought the store brand ready made frozen pie crusts. They were never a match for this pie crust.

When I was young, my mother let us roll out the pie crusts, but she always mixed up the ingredients herself like it was a treasured secret recipe. I think she finally felt sorry for me and gave in and gave me this recipe. I believe it had something to do with that pie I made and brought once to our family Christmas gathering, in which the crust was so awful that you couldn't even cut through it with a fork. So if you don't want to be embarrassed and you want a simple and easy pie crust, then I wholeheartedly recommend this one!

(Makes two 9 inch pie crusts)

Ingredients:

- 2 cups unsifted flour
- 2 tsp. salt
- 12 Tbsp. shortening
- 4 Tbsp. ice water
- 2 Tbsp. cider vinegar

Directions:

1. In a small bowl, combine water with ice cubes and set aside.

2. In a medium sized mixing bowl, combine flour and salt.

3. With pastry blender, blend shortening into flour until mixture resembles small peas.

4. Sprinkle vinegar and ice water over flour mixture and mix until you form a ball. (I found it easier to do this with my hands instead of pastry blender).

5. Lightly flour counter surface or pastry board.

6. Divide dough in half, and roll out onto floured surface to 1/8th inch thickness.

7. Carefully fold rolled out dough in half and place into center of pie pan.

8. Unfold, and spread out and bring up the sides of pan. Fold crust over rim of pie pan and cut off excess crust.

9. Using the tines of a fork or your index finger, make

impressions along the edge of pie crust.

10. If you are using the crust for custard or pudding pies, you will need to poke holes with the end of a fork along the sides and bottom of the crust, and prebake the crust until light golden brown.

Raisin Pie

Truly aromatic while baking and the raisins make this pie truly soporific in taste!

Ingredients:

- 2-8 inch pie crusts
- 1 cup raisins
- 1 cup water
- 2 Tbsp. clear gelatin
- ¼ tsp. salt
- 1 cup sugar
- 1 Tbsp. apple cider vinegar

Directions:

1. Preheat oven to 400°F.

2. Roll out two pie crusts and place one crust inside an 8 inch pie pan.

3. In small bowl, mix together gelatin, salt, sugar, and vinegar to make a thickening.

4. In medium saucepan, cook raisins and water over medium heat for 25 minutes.

5. Add thickening and cook until mixture sticks to spoon.

6. Pour pie filling into pie crust. Cover filling with second pie crust. Cut off excess crust and press down with index finger around rim of pie pan so that the two crusts connect.

7. Make a cross in the center of crust and then place four slits in the top of crust in between the sections of the cross.

8. Bake in preheated oven for 30 minutes.

Classic Mincemeat Pie

This pie was long ago referred to as "mutton pie" or "Christmas pie" and originally had an oblong shape to represent the "coffin of Christ". During the Civil war the Puritans banned this pie, due to its connection to Catholicism.

This pie has been a family favorite for many generations, and I for one am thankful that I did not live during that era and that the ban was done away with. I believe it would have been atrocious not to have been able to taste this sweet and spicy pie.

Ingredients:

- 2- 9 inch rolled-out crusts
- 2- 9 inch pie crusts
- 2 ½ cups peeled, chopped apples
- 1 cup raisins
- ½ cup chopped pecans

- ½ cup currants
- 1 ½ Tsp. grated lemon rind
- 2 ½ cups brown sugar, firmly packed
- ½ cup vinegar
- 2 Tbsp. lemon juice
- ½ cup molasses
- 1 cup apple cider
- 1 ½ Tsp. ground cloves
- 1 ½ Tsp. ground cinnamon
- 1 ½ Tsp. ground nutmeg
- ¾ Tsp. salt
- ¾ Tsp. pepper
- 1 ½ pounds lean ground beef

Directions:

1. In a large Dutch oven, combine apples, raisins, pecans, currants, lemon rind, sugar, vinegar, lemon juice, molasses, and cider.

2. With wooden spoon, mix until well combined.

3. Add in spices, salt and pepper and stir again.

4. Over medium heat, cook mixture for 15 minutes.

5. Add beef and cook for another 15 minutes.

6. Remove from heat and cool mixture for 15 minutes.

7. Preheat oven to 350°F.

8. While mixture is cooling, cut ¾ inch strips from the 2 rolled –out crusts for the top crusts lattice design.

9. Divide the mixture evenly into the 2 pie crust shells.

10. Arrange the lattice design on top of the filling by interlacing the strips.

11. Seal pastry edges together and using your index finger flute the edges.

12. Brush top of pie with egg and sprinkle with sugar.

13. Bake for 55 minutes or until golden brown. Cool completely before serving.

Meringue

An easy meringue to make and tastes good too. This is the recipe I use for all the pies I make that require a meringue. I think you will enjoy it too.

Ingredients:

- 2 Tbsp. Cornstarch
- 12 Tbsp. sugar
- 1 cup water
- ¼ tsp. salt
- 6 egg whites
- 2 Tsp. vanilla

Directions:

1. In small bowl, dissolve cornstarch with water and mix until smooth.

2. In small saucepan, combine cornstarch-water mixture, sugar and salt and bring to a boil.

3. Stirring constantly, boil mixture for 3 minutes. Remove from heat and set aside to cool.

4. In large mixing bowl, beat egg whites until stiff. Add cooled mixture and vanilla and beat for 5 minutes.

5. Place meringue on top of pie and arrange peaks with a spoon.

6. Bake in oven until peaks are golden brown.

7. Remove from heat and allow pie to completely cool before refrigerating.

Cherished Chocolate Meringue Pie

Your family will appreciate the smooth and creamy texture of the chocolate pie filling in this pie. And to top it off, is a wonderful tasting meringue. One taste of this scrumptious pie is all that is needed to make this pie one of your family cherished favorites!

Ingredients:

- 2-9 inch pie crusts
- 2 cups milk
- 1 cup + * Tsp. sugar
- ½ Tsp. salt
- 6 Tbsp. baking cocoa
- 6 eggs
- 4 Tbsp. cornstarch
- 1 stick butter

Directions:

1. Preheat oven to 350°F.

2. Separate eggs and reserve egg whites for meringue.

3. In medium bowl, beat egg yolks. Set aside.

4. Press fork tines into pie crusts on both the sides and the bottom.

5. Bake Pie Crusts until light golden brown. Set aside and cool.

6. In heavy bottomed saucepan over medium heat, melt butter. Remove from heat and add sugar, 1½ cups of the milk, and salt and cocoa.

7. In small bowl, combine remaining milk with cornstarch and beaten egg yolks and mix until smooth.

8. Return saucepan to heat and add in cornstarch mixture.

9. Stirring constantly, cook until thickened pudding consistency.

10. Pour mixture evenly into baked pie shells.

11. Top with meringue and bake until peaks are golden.

Lemony Lemon Meringue Pie

Although lemons are known to be sour, there is nothing sour about this pie. In fact, it is sweet and refreshingly flavorsome.

Ingredients:

- 2-9 inch pie crusts
- 2 cups sugar
- 2/3 cup cornstarch
- ¼ Tsp. salt
- 4 cups cold water
- 4 drops food coloring
- 6 eggs

- 6 Tbsp. butter
- ½ cup fresh lemon juice
- 4 Tsp. grated lemon

Directions:

1. Preheat oven to 350° F. With tines of fork, press holes along sides and bottom of pie shells. Bake pie shells till light golden brown. Remove from oven and set aside.

2. Separate eggs and reserve egg whites for meringue.

3. In medium bowl, beat egg yolks. Set aside.

4. Dissolve cornstarch in the water and mix until smooth.

5. In heavy-bottomed saucepan, combine sugar, cornstarch-water mixture, salt and food coloring.

6. Cook, stirring constantly until mixture thickens to pudding consistency. Add beaten egg yolks to mixture and cook for an additional two minutes, stirring constantly.

7. Remove from heat and add butter, lemon juice, and grated lemon. Stir until mixed well.

8. Pour into baked pie shells and top with meringue.

9. Bake Meringue according to meringue directions.

10. Remove pie from oven and cool completely before refrigerating.

Extremely Palatable Pecan Pie

An extremely tasty Pecan Pie, with an awesome sweet and gooey center and an enjoyable Pecan topping. This pie just cannot be beat when it comes to taste and is usually found at Christmastime at many family gatherings!

Ingredients:

- 2 – 9 inch pie shells
- 2 cups dark corn syrup
- 1 cup sugar
- 6 eggs
- 2 Tsp. vanilla
- 1 ½ sticks of butter
- 1 ½ cups pecan halves

Directions:

1. Preheat oven to 350°F.

2. In medium bowl, beat eggs until fluffy. Set aside.

3. In heavy-bottomed saucepan, mix sugar, syrup, and butter together.

4. Cook over medium heat until butter melts, stirring constantly.

5. Add beaten eggs and vanilla to mixture and cook until mixture begins to bubble and pop.

6. Remove from heat and add ½ off the pecans and mix well.

7. Pour mixture into pie shells. Top pies with remaining pecans.

8. Place pies on baking sheet and bake for 45 minutes to an hour, until golden brown.

First Choice Cherry Pie

These days, people are so busy that they choose to buy a frozen cherry pie and bake it themselves, or they will buy the canned cherry pie filling and slap it inside a store-bought already made pie crust. There's nothing wrong with that, but if I was going to serve a really great and flavorsome cherry pie at Christmas, this pie would definitely be my first choice!

Ingredients:

- 2-9 inch pie shells
- 2- 9 inch crusts, rolled out
- 1 ½ cup granulated sugar
- ½ cup cornstarch
- ½ Tsp. salt
- 8 cups cherries, pitted
- 3 cups water
- 4 Tbsp. lemon juice
- 4 Tbsp. sugar for sprinkling

Directions:

1. Preheat oven to 400°F.

2. In a medium bowl, dissolve cornstarch with water and stir until smooth.

3. In large saucepan, combine water mixture, salt, sugar, and lemon juice. Mix well.

4. Add in cherries.

5. Over medium heat, cook mixture and bring to a boil.

6. Cook and stir for an additional 2 minutes or until mixture thickens. Remove from heat and set aside.

7. Cut rolled-out pastry into ¾ inch strips.

8. Divide mixture evenly into pie shells. Using cut strips, create a lattice crust, and flute edges.

9. Sprinkle granulated sugar over top of pies. Cover the edges loosely with foil.

10. Place pies on baking tray. Bake pies for 20 minutes, remove foil from edges, and bake for an additional 15-20 minutes or until crust is golden in color and filling has bubbled.

Amazing Apple Pie

This Apple Pie is truly amazing in taste and sensuous to the nostrils. The taste of baked apples spiced with cinnamon is absolutely incredible, and there is nothing as comforting as the smell of a baked apple pie on a wintery day!

Makes 2 Pies

Ingredients:

- 2-9 inch pie shells
- 2- 9 inch rolled-out pie crusts
- 16 Golden Delicious Apples, cored, peeled, and sliced
- 2 Tsp. cinnamon
- 1 Tsp. salt
- 2-12 oz. cans frozen apple juice
- 6 Tbsp. cornstarch
- 2 ¼ cup sugar
- 1 cup brown sugar

- 4 Tbsp. butter

Directions:

1. Preheat oven to 350°F.

2. In a large skillet, combine apples, cinnamon, salt, and 1 can of apple juice. Simmer apples until transparent.

3. Mix cornstarch with second can of apple juice.

4. Add cornstarch mixture, sugars, and butter to simmered apples and continue cooking, stirring constantly until mixture thickens.

5. Divide mixture evenly into unbaked pie shells.

6. Place rolled-out crusts on top of apple filling and trim excess along edges.

7. Flute edges of pie to connect crusts. With a knife, cut a 2 inch cross in center of pie, and cut 2 inch vented slices in between cross.

8. Place pies on baking sheet and bake for 45 minutes or until top crust is golden brown and filling is bubbly.

Perfectly Pleasant Pumpkin Roll

I have a niece who makes this pumpkin roll and brings it every year to our family Christmas gathering. She makes hers from scratch and uses fresh pumpkin pulp from pumpkins she grows in her garden. This recipe is a little bit easier to make since you can make it from canned pumpkin. Regardless of whether you choose to use fresh pumpkin pulp or canned pumpkin, the taste of this pumpkin roll will be perfectly pleasant to your palate!

Ingredients:

- 3 large eggs
- 1 cup sugar
- 1 Tsp. baking soda
- ¾ cup flour
- 2/3 cup pumpkin
- 3 Tbsp. butter
- 8 oz. cream cheese, room temperature
- ¾ Tsp. vanilla
- 2 cup powdered sugar
- Wax paper
- Tea towel or cotton linen

Directions:

1. Preheat oven to 375°F.

2. In large mixing bowl, mix eggs, granulated sugar, soda, flour and pumpkin until well combined and smooth.

3. Line a 10 x 15 pan with wax paper and grease or spray wax paper.

4. Roll out towel and sprinkle with ¾ cup powdered sugar.

5. Pour batter into pan and bake for 15 minutes.

6. Turn out onto towel. Remove wax paper and roll up while still hot.

7. Let set for 20 minutes.

8. In medium bowl, mix together butter, cream cheese, vanilla and 1 cup powdered sugar until smooth.

9. Unroll cake, spread on cream mixture and re-roll. Sprinkle top with more powdered sugar.

10. Refrigerate for at least 1 hour or until ready to serve.

Can't Be Beat Banana Pudding

I have made this Banana Pudding so many times, and still my husband swears that it isn't as good as my Mothers Banana Pudding. I use the same recipe that my Mother uses, and she swears that she has included every ingredient in the recipe. I think he just says it to butter her up so she will make one just for him at Christmas to insure that he will get some, because it is so creamy and delicious that there is usually none left by the time he reaches the dessert table.

Ingredients:

- 4 cups milk
- 2 cup sugar
- 8 Tbsp. cornstarch
- 12 Tbsp. butter
- 8 ripened bananas cut in slices
- 1 Tsp. vanilla
- 1 tub whipped cream
- 1 box Vanilla wafers

Directions:

1. In a heavy-bottomed saucepan, over medium heat, melt butter.

2. Dissolve the cornstarch in ½ cup milk and stir till smooth.

3. Add sugar, remainder of the milk, cornstarch mix and the salt. Cook until thick and clear.

4. Stir in bananas and vanilla, remove from heat, and set aside to cool.

5. With rolling pin, crush ½ of the Vanilla wafers. Line them on the bottom of a 9 x 11 baking pan.

6. Stand some of the wafers on end around the sides of the baking pan.

7. Pour cooled pudding into pan. Cover with foil or lid and refrigerate for an hour.

8. Uncover pudding and top with whipped cream, return to refrigerator until ready to serve.

Mammas Seventy Five Dollar Persimmon Pudding

This baked creamy and rich tasting Persimmon Pudding will stimulate your taste buds, while the aroma will stimulate your nostrils. My Mothers Persimmon Pudding is so delicious that it has been auctioned off at her Church with the winning bidder willing to pay as much as $75.00 for this delightful treat. It has been said that it was well worth the price that was paid, it's just that good!

Ingredients:

- 2 cups sugar
- 2 cups persimmon pulp
- 2 eggs
- 1 cup buttermilk
- 1 cup sweet milk
- 1 tsp. soda
- 2 tsp. baking powder
- 2 heaping tsp. cinnamon
- 2 cups flour

- ¼ cup butter, melted

Directions:

1. Preheat oven to 350°F.

2. In a large bowl, mix together sugar, persimmon pulp, eggs, buttermilk, and sweet milk. Beat with mixer until well combined.

3. Add remaining ingredients and mix well.

4. Grease a 9 x 13 baking pan with butter.

5. Pour mixture into pan and bake for 30-35 minutes, until top is slightly browned.

6. Remove from oven and cool on wire rack. Pudding will drop after cooling.

7. Can serve either warm or cold. Top with whipped cream when serving.

Irresistible Cherry Jubilee

This Cherry Jubilee is so irresistible that you will need a lot of self control in order to resist going back for a second helping. Made with a rich and sweet cherry filling, crushed chocolate crème cookies, cream cheese and whipped crème, your taste sensations will think that they are a part of a grand jubilee.

Ingredients:

- 1 ½ cup granulated sugar
- ½ cup cornstarch
- ½ Tsp. salt
- 8 cups cherries, pitted
- 3 cups water
- 4 Tbsp. lemon juice
- 1 package of Oreos or chocolate crème cookies
- 1 (8 oz.) pkg. cream cheese
- 1 carton Cool Whip
- 1 cup sugar
- 1 tsp. vanilla

Directions:

1. In a medium bowl, dissolve cornstarch with water and stir until smooth.

2. In large saucepan, combine water mixture, salt, sugar, and lemon juice. Mix well.

3. Add in cherries.

4. Over medium heat, cook mixture and bring to a boil.

5. Cook and stir for an additional 2 minutes or until mixture thickens. Remove from heat and set aside.

6. In medium bowl, cream together cream cheese, sugar, and vanilla. Set aside.

7. Place ½ of the cookies in large Ziploc bag, and push out air as you zip the bag. Using the end of a glass, crush cookies.

8. Line the bottom of a 9x13 pan with crushed cookies.

9. Top the layer of cookies with crème mixture, spreading it out evenly.

10. Place the remaining cookies in the bag and crush them. Reserve ¼ cup of crushed cookies and sprinkle the rest of the crushed cookies over the crème mixture.

11. Pour cherry filling on top of crushed cookies and spread out evenly.

12. Cover with plastic wrap or lid and refrigerate for an hour.

13. Remove lid and spread Cool Whip over top of cherry filling. Sprinkle reserved crushed cookies over top.

14. Return to refrigerator until ready to serve.

Over The Top Red Velvet Cake

This cake is smooth and velvety on your tongue. It is also rich in flavor and its royal dark reddish color makes this cake an elegant attraction on your dessert table.

Ingredients:

Cake:

- 1 ½ cup sugar
- ½ cup butter
- 2 eggs
- 1 Tsp. vanilla
- 2 oz. red food coloring
- 2 ½ cups flour
- 1 Tsp. baking soda
- 1 Tbsp. cocoa
- 1 cup buttermilk
- 1 tsp. vinegar

Icing:

- 4 ½ Tbsp. flour
- 1 cup milk
- 1 ½ sticks butter
- 1 ½ cups sugar
- 3 Tbsp. vanilla
- 4 ½ Tbsp. shortening

Directions:

1. Preheat oven to 350°F. Grease and flour (3) 8-inch round cake pans.

2. In large mixing bowl, cream sugar and butter and beat till fluffy.

3. Add eggs one at a time, add vanilla and food coloring and mix well.

4. Sift together flour, soda and cocoa in a medium bowl.

5. Gradually add flour mixture to creamed mixture, alternating with buttermilk. Mix well.

6. Fold in vinegar.

7. Pour into prepared baking pans. Bake for 35 minutes. Remove from oven and cool completely.

8. In medium saucepan, cook flour and milk until thick; set aside to cool.

9. In medium bowl, cream together butter, sugar and vanilla.

10. When flour mixture has cooled, add butter mixture and beat until consistency of whipped cream.

11. Place one cake layer onto cake plate and spread icing over top. Repeat process with remaining cakes. Ice top and sides of cake.

12. Place cake inside cake carrier or on a cake stand that has a cover to keep fresh. Cake does not need to be refrigerated.

Colorful Christmas Cake

I love to watch the expressions that the Children have on their faces when an adult cuts into this cake. It already looks appetizing before it has been cut, but to a child the best part seems to be the colorful surprise that appears on the inside. Not only is this cake attractive, but it is scrumptious as well.

Ingredients:

- 1 cup butter
- 4 cups sugar
- 4 eggs
- 4 Tsp. vanilla
- 3 cups flour
- 3Tsp. baking powder
- 1 cup milk
- 1-3 oz. pkg. of Cherry flavored gelatin
- 1-3 oz. pkg. of Lime flavored gelatin
- 2 cups boiling water
- 2 tubs whipped topping
- 1 jar maraschino cherries
- 3 mint leaves (optional)

Directions:

1. Preheat oven to 350°F. Grease and flour (3) 8 inch round cake pans.

2. In a large mixing bowl, cream sugar and butter. Add eggs to cream mixture one at a time and then add vanilla.

3. Add flour and baking powder and mix well.

4. Add milk to mixture and beat until smooth.

5. Divide mixture by pouring mixture into pans as evenly as possible. Bake for 35 – 40 minutes or until cake springs back when touched.

6. Remove from oven and place on wire rack to cool completely.

7. When cake has cooled, use an ice pick or knife and poke holes into cakes.

8. In small bowl, mix lime gelatin with 1 cup boiling hot water.

9. In small bowl, mix cherry gelatin with 1 cup boiling hot water.

10. Slowly pour gelatins over top of cake. (I will pour red gelatin over top around the edge of cake in a two inch radius, and then pour green in the center. I then reverse the colors for the second layer, and then repeat the process of the first layer for the remaining cake.)

11. Let cakes set for 20 minutes. After time has elapsed, place 1st layer on cake plate and cover with whipped topping. Repeat process for remaining layers and then frost sides with whipped topping.

12. Drain cherries.

13. Arrange the mint leaves on top and then place cherries in center of cake.

14. Place cake in cake carrier or cake holder. Refrigerate until ready to serve.

Z-licious Zucchini Bread

When it is summertime and we are out picking all the zucchini that we have grown in our garden, there is no question as to what we are going to do with it all. The answer is quite simple. We are going to grate it, put it up in freezer bags and freeze it so we can enjoy this marvelous tasting zucchini bread at Christmastime.

Ingredients:

- 1 cup vegetable oil
- 1 Tsp. vanilla
- 3 eggs
- 1 cup water
- 1 Tsp. cinnamon
- 1 Tsp. salt
- 1 Tsp. baking soda
- 1 Tsp. baking powder
- 2 cups sugar

- 3 cups flour
- 2 cups grated zucchini

Directions:

1. Preheat oven to 350°F. Grease a large bread pan.

2. In a large mixing bowl, mix together oil, vanilla, eggs, and water.

3. Add cinnamon, salt, baking soda and powder, sugar and flour and mix until well combined.

4. Using a wooden spoon, mix in grated zucchini.

5. Pour into prepared pan. Bake for 30 minutes or until toothpick inserted into center comes out clean.

6. Place on wire rack to cool. Remove from pan and wrap with foil or plastic wrap.

Best Ever Banana Nut Bread

The name says it all, and it is the best Banana nut bread that I have ever had. It is extremely moist and the walnuts make this bread such a delightful treat.

Ingredients:

- 4 ripe bananas (best when the peeling has begun to turn black)
- 1 egg
- ¼ cup melted butter
- 1 ½ Tsp. vanilla
- 1 ¼ cup sugar
- 1 ½ cups all purpose flour
- 1 Tsp. baking soda
- ½ Tsp. salt
- ¼ cup chopped walnuts

Directions:

1. Preheat oven to 350°F. Grease a loaf pan.

2. In a large mixing bowl, using a potato masher, mash bananas.

3. Add eggs, butter, and vanilla and beat with mixer for 1 minute or until well combined.

4. Add sugar, flour, soda, and salt to mixture and mix until flour is absorbed.

5. Stir in walnuts. Pour into prepared loaf pan and bake for 1 hour or until toothpick inserted into center comes out clean.

6. Place on wire rack to cool. Remove from pan and wrap with foil or plastic wrap.

Christmas Buffet

It has been said that the best present you can ever give someone is your time, and I firmly believe that is true. Growing up, my best recollections are the hours my Mother spent in the kitchen preparing the Christmas meals. It didn't begin on Christmas morning; it began at least a week before Christmas. During this time, she worked a full time job, took care of five kids who were still living at home, and baked goodies non stop.

Many years have passed and a lot of things have changed since those days. One thing however has never changed. A lot of work, time and love still go into the meals that we serve at Christmas. Mom started a new Christmas Tradition when she decided that we would get together somewhere besides the old homestead twenty eight years ago.

That Christmas Tradition has continued on through two more generations and hopingly will continue long after we are all gone. The meals seem to get bigger with every generation and now we have to set the food up buffet style. It now requires three eight foot tables just for the food.

We have kept to the same menu every year but because our family has grown, it takes more food. I guess we kept the same menu because these foods are our favorites and must have foods at our Christmas Buffet.

So far no one has dared to err or change the menu. Maybe someday, someone in a future generation will add something new to the menu. And although a lot of love and work still goes into preparing these Christmas recipes, our generation has benefited from the ability to purchase the ingredients at our local grocery.

Below is the Christmas menu for our family gathering.

- Glazed Ham
- Homemade Chicken and Dumplings
- Homemade Beef and Noodles
- Turkey with Sage Dressing
- Swedish Meatballs
- Homemade Yeast Rolls
- Mashed Potatoes
- Turkey Gravy
- Sweet Potatoes
- Potato Salad
- Broccoli Salad
- Lovely Layered Salad
- Tossed Salad
- Cole Slaw
- Raisin Salad
- Ambrosia
- Waldorf salad
- Green Beans
- Baked Beans
- Sweet Corn
- Deviled Eggs
- Cranberry Relish

As you can plainly see, we like our food and we enjoy having a variety. Ever year though, I ask myself "where will I find room for my dessert?" I guess this is why my whole family is a large family in more ways than one.

I haven't included all the recipes for every one of the foods listed above, but I covered the ones that I knew you would enjoy making. I hope you will allow your children to help you in the preparation of these foods.

Although these foods are really great, even greater yet is the time we spend with our children making memories that will last a lifetime. And that my friend is the best recipe you can hand down to the next generation!

Glorious Glazed Ham

A really sweet and delectable glazed ham made from maraschino cherries, pineapple slices and brown sugar.

Ingredients:

- 1 large precooked Ham shank or butt
- ½ cup brown sugar
- 2 Tbsp. corn starch
- 2 Tsp. prepared mustard
- Whole cloves
- ½ cup pineapple juice (reserved from canned pineapple)
- 1 can pineapple slices
- 1 jar maraschino cherries
- 2 Tbsp. butter
- Box of wooden toothpicks

Directions:

1. Preheat oven to 375°F.

2. Drain juice from pineapple and reserve juice. Drain cherries. Set aside.

3. In a small bowl, mix together cornstarch with juice and stir till smooth.

4. In medium saucepan, combine brown sugar, mustard, butter, and cornstarch mix.

5. Over medium heat, cook mixture stirring constantly until thickened.

6. Remove from heat and set aside.

7. Place ham fat side up in 13x9x2 inch baking pan.

8. Brush ½ of glaze mixture over top of ham. Arrange pineapple slices around ham, press cloves into ham just underneath center of pineapple ring to secure them.

9. Run a toothpick through cherry and insert into ham leaving enough of the toothpick showing above the cherry for easy removal once ham has been baked.

10. Make an aluminum tent over ham and bake for 45 minutes. Remove from oven and cover ham with remaining glaze. Bake uncovered for 20 more minutes or remaining time according to baking directions for size of ham.

Creamy Chicken and Fluffy Drop Dumplings

Believe me, if this Creamy Chicken and Fluffy Drop Dumplings could not be found anywhere on the table at our Christmas gathering, there would be a lot of grumbling and disappointed people. These moist and fluffy drop dumplings cooked in a creamy sauce that was produced from the chicken stock are a family favorite, and each Christmas we look forward to eating our fair share of them.

Ingredients:

- 1 large whole chicken
- 4 Tbsp. corn starch
- 2 cups flour
- 1 Tsp. salt
- 1 Tbsp. black pepper
- ¼ Tsp. baking soda
- 2 Tsp. baking powder
- ½ Tbsp. shortening
- 1 cup buttermilk
- 1 egg

Directions:

1. In large stockpot, cover chicken with at least 6 cups of water, add salt and pepper, and cook until chicken falls away from the bone.

2. Remove from heat.

3. Using a strainer with a large bowl or pot underneath,

separate the broth from chicken. Reserve broth.

4. Debone chicken and cut up into bite size pieces. Set aside.

5. In large mixing bowl, combine flour, baking soda and powder. Mix well.

6. In small bowl, combine shortening, buttermilk, and egg. Beat until well combined.

7. Add egg mixture to flour mixture and mix well. Dough will be sticky. Set aside.

8. Using the same stockpot that you cooked your chicken in, pour all but ¼ cup of the reserved broth back in and bring to a boil.

9. Mix cornstarch with ¼ cup broth until smooth. Set aside.

10. When broth begins to boil, begin dropping dumpling mixture into broth by using a soup spoon.

11. Dumplings will cook and rise to top of broth. When they begin to do this, gently move them out of the way with a wooden spoon as you continue to drop the remaining dumplings.

12. Lower heat, add cornstarch mixture and chicken and cook for additional 15 minutes. Stir occasionally to keep dumplings from sticking or scorching.

Bodacious Beef and Noodles

When I was growing up, Sunday was the day in which my Mother cooked a large meal. Her Homemade Beef and Noodles were always something to look forward too. She browned the beef first in a skillet and used the drippings to make dark rich gravy. Her noodles were always perfect and tender, and never tough or chewy. I have never found Beef and Noodles that are as delicious as these.

Ingredients:

- 3 pounds chuck roast, cut into 1 inch cubes
- ½ stick butter
- 2 Tbsp. browning sauce (Kitchen Bouquet or Gravy Master)
- 2 ¼ Tsp. salt
- 2 Tsp. pepper
- ½ Tsp. seasoned salt
- 5 cups water
- 3 cups flour
- 3 eggs
- 3 Tbsp. milk

Directions:

1. In a large bowl, pour in flour and make a well in center. Drop eggs, milk, and ¼ Tsp. salt into center.

2. Using your hands and starting from the center, mix flour with the liquid until stiff dough has formed.

3. Lightly dust a large area on counter or pastry sheet with flour. Pour out dough onto floured surface and push down using the palms of your hands.

4. Using a floured rolling pin, start in middle of dough and roll outward on all sides to a 1/16 inch thickness. Lightly dust top of dough with flour and roll into log. Cut ½ inch wide strips into log.

5. Picking up one strip at a time, place noodles onto a drying rack. Dry for 1 hour and then turn noodles over. After noodles have been turned over, dry for another hour.

6. In a large skillet, melt butter over medium heat. Add beef to skillet along with browning sauce, salts and pepper. Brown the meat, stirring occasionally to brown all sides. Add water to cover meat and cook until tender.

7. Remove meat from skillet and pour broth into large stockpot. Bring broth to a boil and drop noodles into broth. Cook until tender, stirring occasionally to keep from sticking.

Note: You can use a clean oven rack for a drying rack.

Succulent Swedish Meatballs

If I had to travel all the way to Sweden just to get some of these succulent Swedish meatballs, I would.

These meatballs are moist, filled with my favorite spices, and slowly cooked in a delightful tasting cream sauce.

Ingredients:

Meatballs:

- 4 slices white bread
- ½ cup half and half
- 1 ½ pound ground beef
- 1 ½ pound sausage
- 1 onion, finely chopped
- 2 eggs
- ¼ Tsp. ground allspice

- ½ Tsp. ground cardamom
- ¼ Tsp. ground ginger
- ½ Tsp. granulated garlic powder
- ½ Tsp. salt
- ½ Tsp. pepper
- 4 Tbsp. vegetable oil

Cream Sauce:

- 4 cups beef broth
- 4 Tbsp. water
- 4 Tbsp. flour
- ½ cup heavy cream
- ½ Tsp. onion powder
- ½ Tsp. garlic powder
- ½ Tsp. salt
- ½ Tsp. pepper

Directions:

1. Remove crust from bread and tear bread into small pieces. Soak bread in half and half until bread is soft.

2. In a large bowl, combine meat, onion, eggs and spices. Add soaked bread and mix until evenly combined.

3. Shape meat mixture into golf size balls.

4. In a heavy skillet, add oil and place meatballs leaving enough room to turn them. Brown meatballs on all sides. Remove meatballs from skillet and place in 7 quart Crockpot on medium setting.

5. In the same skillet, pour in ½ of the beef broth and simmer for a few minutes while scraping the bottom of skillet to remove any debris that has stuck to bottom of skillet.

6. Place a strainer over another saucepan and strain the stock from the debris. Pour in the remaining broth. Bring to a boil.

7. In a small bowl, mix flour with water until smooth.

8. Remove broth from heat. Add remaining ingredients to broth including flour mixture. Stir until mixed well. Pour mixture over meatballs. Turn Crockpot down to low setting and simmer in Crockpot until ready to serve.

Note: Can also be cooked in large skillet with lid, but be sure to stir often to keep from sticking.

Doubly Yummy Yeast Rolls

I absolutely love the aroma of yeast rolls baking in the oven. There is something really comforting about that aroma. But I must say that even though these rolls smell so great when baking, I love the taste of them even more.

Ingredients:

- 3 pkg. dry yeast
- ¾ cup warm water
- 1½ cups scalded milk
- ¾ cup melted butter
- ¾ cup sugar
- 3 eggs beaten
- 9 cups flour
- 1 ½ Tsp. Salt

Directions:

1. Dissolve yeast in warm water and set aside.

2. In a large bowl, combine cooled milk, butter, sugar, salt and eggs and mix with mixer.

3. Add yeast and water mixture and half of flour and mix on medium speed for 2 minutes. Add remaining flour and stir until smooth. Dough will be soft.

4. Form dough into ball and place on floured surface and knead well. Place dough in greased bowl and turn until ball has been greased on all sides. Cover bowl with damp towel and let rise for 1 hour.

5. Grease a 9x13 baking pan. Punch dough down and form into 2 inch dough balls. Place dough balls in prepared pan, side by side. Cover with damp towel and let rise until doubled.

6. Bake at 350°F until golden brown, approximately 20 minutes. Remove from oven and brush tops with butter while still hot.

Lovely Layered Salad

This layered salad is lovely to look at and really enticing with all its colorful ingredients. It also has a very lovely taste to boot!

Ingredients:

- 1 head of Iceberg lettuce, chopped
- 1 head broccoli, cut up into small pieces
- 1 head cauliflower, cut up in small pieces
- 1 bag frozen peas
- 1 large red onion, chopped
- 2 cups mayonnaise
- 3 Tbsp. sugar
- 1 pound bacon, crisply cooked and broke into pieces
- 1-16 oz. pkg. cheddar cheese

Directions:

1. In a small bowl, combine mayonnaise with sugar. Set aside.

2. In a large glass bowl or 9 x 13 glass baking dish, place chopped lettuce and spread out.

3. Layer broccoli on top of lettuce.

4. Layer cauliflower on top of broccoli.

5. Layer peas on top of cauliflower.

6. Layer red onion on top of peas.

7. Spread mayonnaise mix over onion.

8. Sprinkle bacon pieces over mayonnaise mix.

9. Cover bacon with cheese.

10. Cover with lid or plastic wrap.

11. Refrigerate overnight and keep refrigerated until ready to serve.

Wonderful and Fruity Waldorf Salad

This Waldorf salad has been a family favorite for many years. This salad is made with a variety of apples and full of walnuts and pecans. It can always be found at our Christmas family gathering. It is also a great way for us to use up all the apples and the nuts from the fruit baskets that we receive at Christmas!

Ingredients:

- 3 Golden delicious apples, skins left on and cored
- 3 Gala apples, skins left on and cored
- 3 Jonathan apples, skins left on and cored
- 3 celery stalks, chopped
- 2 cups seedless grapes, halved
- 1 cup chopped pecans
- 1 cup chopped walnuts
- 1 cup raisins
- ½ cup shredded coconut

- 1 ½ cup mayonnaise
- 4 Tbsp. sugar

Directions:

1. In a small bowl, mix together mayonnaise and sugar.

2. In a large bowl, combine the remaining ingredients and mix until evenly combined.

3. Stir in mayonnaise mix and mix well.

4. Cover with lid or plastic wrap and chill until ready to serve.

Best Ever Broccoli Salad

There are many variations of Broccoli Salad, but I like this one best. The sweet and tangy Lemon Poppy Seed Dressing adds a unique and delightful taste, making it the best broccoli salad I have ever tasted.

Ingredients:

- 4 Tbsp. apple cider vinegar
- 3 Tsp. lemon juice
- 3 Tsp. Dijon mustard
- 3 Tsp. honey
- 3 Tbsp. poppy seeds
- ½ cup sugar
- 1/3 cup vegetable oil
- 1 head of broccoli, cut up
- 1 cup raisins
- 3 carrots, shredded
- 1 pkg. ramen noodles, broke up
- 1 medium onion, diced

Directions:

1. In a medium bowl, combine vinegar, lemon juice, mustard, honey, sugar, oil, and poppy seeds. Mix well. Set aside.

2. In large bowl, combine broccoli, raisins, carrots, ramen noodles, and onion. Mix until evenly combined.

3. Pour liquid mixture over broccoli mixture and stir until evenly distributed.

4. Cover with lid and refrigerate overnight. Keep refrigerated until ready to serve.